I0162466

Father–Daughter Conversations

Dads Love This Book!

"I loved the honesty that each of these fathers offered in their father–daughter conversations. As I read I felt like I was sitting down to have my own conversation with each of these fathers in the hopes that I might capture some wisdom for raising my own daughter. And there's plenty of wisdom to be had. One of the best parts of this book are the questions at the end of each conversation. They equip you to read this book at your leisure or as part of a group of dads where you can start to have real conversations about what it takes to raise our daughters well."

— Bruce Pagano II, TheWholeMan.co

"I totally relate to Jason's story and the wisdom it holds. I was also a 27-year-old new father chasing a dream. But I shifted gears too fast and was fired from my engineering job. With my wife and 9-month-old at home and no job, we were buried under six figures of debt. Don't do it that way! Follow Jason's model of gratitude, patience, and execution."

— Ken Carfagno, Founder of Dadnamics.com
Author of *Arctic Land*

"We hear so much about boys being raised without dads and the implications that result. That's a real problem, and our society is trying to address the influences of role models in their lives and how we can become better at validating our young men.

But what about girls? It's often hard for a man to understand the mind of a woman, but to be blessed with the opportunity of raising one is another story. We've all seen the repercussions of girls who were never validated as women by their own dads.

Our daughters want to know they're beautiful. They wants to know they're loved—that they're special. They want to see themselves twinkle in someone's eye. As dads, we have more power to give her this validation than any other human being.

Through us, our daughters have the opportunity to witness the love of a father, and the love of their Heavenly Father. As you raise your daughter to be the God-fearing woman you want her to be, Father–Daughter Conversations will help you in your journey."

— Robert de Brus, ExperimentalFreedom.com

Free Bonus

As a special thank you for buying a copy of *Father–Daughter Conversations*, I would like to offer you the complete audio book of *Father–Daughter Conversations* 100 percent FREE.

Enjoy! And thank you for helping to change this world by changing yourself. Download your free copy at:

FatherDaughterConversationsBook.com

Father–Daughter Conversations

by Jason Pockrandt

with these amazing dads:

Tommy Maloney
James Woosley
Rob Azevedo
Adam Wernecke
Marcus Kusi
Sean Ackerman
John Wernecke
Josh Rivers
Greg Gamache
Desmond Bibbs

Disclaimer: The information in this book is intended for informational purposes only. I am not a therapist, counselor, or doctor. I am a coach. I provide a safe space for you to self-explore. I firmly believe that you are 100 percent creative, resourceful, and whole. You are not broken or damaged, and you hold all of the answers to your life's questions. This book is my gift to you as a guiding tool to help you self-explore the uniqueness that you are so that you may join me as a father living a legacy worth leaving.

The information in this book is based on the opinions, knowledge, and experience of the authors. Users of this guide are advised to do their own due diligence when making any and all business and life decisions. All information, products, and services that have been provided and presented should be verified by your own qualified professionals. By reading this guide you agree that the author is not responsible for the success or failure of any business decisions related to any information presented within this book.

Father–Daughter Conversations
Copyright 2015 by Jason Pockrandt & Live To Give
Contributing authors retain the copyright to their chapters.

All rights reserved. This publication may not be reproduced, stored, or transmitted in whole or in part, by any means electronic, mechanical, or otherwise without prior written consent from the publisher and the author. Brief quotations may be used in review. All trademarks and registered trademarks appearing in this book are the property of their respective owners.

ISBN-13: 978-0692701003
ISBN-10: 0692701001

Cover Photos by Chandra Pockrandt, ChandraRaePhotography.com
Layout by James Woosley, JamesWoosley.com

Table of Contents

Dedication

To my sweet baby Lenox

I prayed so long asking God to bring me a wife and child. God answered those prayers, and I wrote this book as you turned one year old.

Still, my tears have continued to fall for the loss of my dad, your Grandpa Dean, who you'll never meet. As I look at your beautiful face, all I want is to be the father he couldn't be—and the father I was created to be. Not for me, but for you.

As you grow and those magical days arise when you need to share your heart I only ask one question: Will you open the bedroom door so we can have our *father–daughter conversations*?

— Jason Pockrandt

Foreword

From the time your daughter is born one thing's for sure: she will hang onto your every word. Your words will give her courage in times of fear, comfort in times of stress, and assurance in times of doubt. It will be your words that will make her feel loved when the world tries to tear her down.

In many ways, the words of a father are like oxygen. The moment we stop speaking words of love and affirmation, your child is deprived of the very thing that allows them to live and breathe.

A father's words are life. This book is power packed with principles that can enhance any father–daughter relationship. Today, it's time to sit down and have a conversation with your daughter.

— Brian Pruitt
Founder of PowerofDad.org

Introduction

Let's face it fathers, we often know very little as we embark on the journey of raising our daughters. We are provided with an onslaught of books, quotes, movies, and stories that tell us to "raise a warrior" and "teach your son how to be a man. Search, conquer, and destroy." These are the messages men hear throughout their lives.

So what happens when we become fathers not of sons but of daughters? Society doesn't tell us how to raise girls.

No one took the time out of his busy macho-man life to be a little tender and share with us what it's really like to raise a daughter. No one has told us what it means to have authentic father–daughter conversations or what we need to know to raise a woman of God, a woman who loves, respects, and values herself.

In the pages that follow, 10 successful fathers

join me to share some of the wisdom they've gained along the way. They talk about how they raised their daughters, the lessons they learned, the struggles they faced, and the wisdom they wished they had known when they were new fathers of daughters.

Whether you lack a fatherly role model or you're overwhelmed by the idea of raising a daughter, *Father–Daughter Conversations* was written to fill that void.

Perhaps some of you were like me and lost your father at an early age. Perhaps your dad abandoned the family and your mother raised you alone. Maybe you didn't have any sisters and don't have the slightest clue about women or what young girls even want in life.

This book has been written to give you a behind-the-scenes look into some of those issues while offering sound advice on raising daughters. You'll read these fathers' deepest heartfelt messages for the daughters they have, hold, and love, so that you may find the strength and courage to become the father you were created to be. In turn, you'll be inspired to give your daughters the love they truly need to become the women they were created to be.

My Story

I am Jason Pockrandt. My father passed away when I was 17. I had no one left in my life to share the kinds of lessons found in this book. I had to spend the next eight years of my life struggling to feel worthy enough to become the person I was meant to be.

I spent five years in college, hiding from the reality of being a fatherless son. I graduated with $19,000 in student debt and landed a job I hated in a field I wanted nothing to do with. Two years later, I hit rock bottom.

I had been alone with my thoughts and feelings night after night at this job for far too long. I reconnected with God and took a leap of faith. I transitioned out of darkness and into the light.

I found a personal coach and discovered my own self-worth. I rediscovered what it meant to be the man I had become. I soon began my own journey of rediscovery.

A short two weeks later, I had launched my business, Live To Give, claimed my first coaching client and was feeling more alive than I had ever felt before.

Soon after, I got married to my wonderful wife. At the age of 28, I was blessed beyond measure when my amazingly beautiful daughter Lenox Jane was born.

Today, I serve others as a transformation coach, guiding fatherless fathers in their journeys to become the best fathers they can be, and helping them live a legacy worthy of their families and communities.

I have found some of life's greatest lessons by living through some of life's lowest moments. For me, rock bottom was my trampoline to the life I desired to live, to the husband I wanted to be, and to the father I am today. I am honored to share my lessons learned with you so that you can avoid the potholes I fell into.

Are you ready to change your life?

Right now, you could be wondering if you understand yourself enough to be the father your daughter needs.

The truth is most men don't know how to handle girls. We spent most of our lives trying to figure out the women we knew in high school and college and now the one whose hand we have taken for life in a little thing called marriage.

Make no mistake. Take these words to heart and know firsthand the power they will have on your life by becoming a more authentic, present, loving, caring, and beloved father. Your daughter will melt in your arms as a baby and will cherish each moment she spends with dad as a teenager and young woman.

Having a daughter is not easy. In fact, it will probably be the most difficult adventure you face as a man. But men want to live an adventure! We want a beauty to rescue and a mountain to climb. Allow your daughter to be that beauty, and let the challenge of raising her be the mountain you climb. Enjoy every step of the trek upwards, and keep your eyes on the prize: a beautiful woman proud to call you Dad.

Most fathers I coach are self-proclaimed introverts, and feel that the only people they can talk to are their wives or God. There's nothing wrong with that. Unfortunately, they're often afraid to ask questions and seek the help they need.

I know the feeling. I also was too self-reliant and too stubborn to ask for help. I was content to learn things the hard way. That's why I compiled this book of stories for you. I hope it helps you learn from other fathers, and serves as a safe place to let go of any self-doubt you have about being a father.

As you read this book, answer the questions at the end of each chapter. Tap into knowledge and power that you already have.

Here is my promise to you. If you stick with it to the end, I guarantee you will reevaluate the way you view your life and your daughter. You will transform the relationship you have with her for the better, and the two of you will become closer. And you will have gained wisdom that will serve you for decades to come.

DO NOT continue to be the father who puts in 60 hours a week, brings a fat paycheck home, buys his daughter fancy clothes and a new car, and thinks life is perfect only to wake up and realize that you never gave what she really wanted: love and attention, time and space with her father.

Be the man she admires, the one she looks up to, the father who shapes her worldview.

— Jason Pockrandt

Oh My God.
I'm Going to Be a Dad?

by Jason Pockrandt

*A man is not complete
until he has seen the baby he has made.*

—Sammy Davis Jr.

*We never know the love of a parent
until we become parents ourselves.*

—Henry Ward Beecher

I have a confession to make. There are times when I struggle to take care of my household while I chase my dreams. I struggle at times to be the man I need to be for my family and myself.

Have you felt that way before? I think we've all faced times of trial and doubt when we first begin the journey of being a father, wondering if we are on the right path and making the right moves—if the choices and the directions we take are the right ones. Oftentimes, we feel impatient and start moving faster than we should.

Several years ago, my wife and I felt that way. We were impatient, feeling as if life was too slow for us and that God wasn't giving us enough of what we wanted. That's about the time I discovered that God has a very good sense of humor!

It was April of 2014. I was 27 years old at the time, and my world was about to be shaken. The best miracle I could have ever received came at the perfect time in our lives when our patience was wearing thin and our dreams were ever evolving.

I was working full-time at Target, while trying to build a coaching business that wasn't taking off as fast as I wanted.

Although I'd lost my own father years earlier, I would lay awake in bed at night, dreaming of the day I would be a father. I wanted the life and love that I never experienced. So I did what I thought made the most sense. I quit my job and walked out of Target on April 29th, 2014, in order to follow my dreams of becoming a full time life coach and speaker.

Two months later, my wife and I found out she was pregnant with our first child. At first, I didn't know what to think. I couldn't feel a thing. I was scared. I was excited. I was ready to cry.

My initial response was, "Oh my God! I'm going to be a dad?"

That's when reality hit me. I was now in the spotlight. I would soon have the eyes of an angel staring up at me, asking for my love. But what had I done?

I had just walked away from a full-time job. I thought I was doing right by going all in on my dreams. But I wondered if we'd be able to make ends meet or put food on the table.

Maybe the home pregnancy test wasn't right, I thought. *There's a chance it could be a false positive.*

Then again, we had taken three pregnancy tests—and all three had been positive. Just in case, we decided to schedule an appointment with my wife's doctor for another test.

The wait for those final results seemed like the longest of our lives.

When the door finally cracked open, the doctor walked in with a smile on her face.

"Congratulations," she said, looking at me.

"For what?" I asked.

She looked at my wife and said, "You're pregnant."

"Yay!" was all I could muster. A smile came across my face, even though her announcement scared me at the same time.

It was a lot like the walk down the wedding aisle. Just as that day marked the end of my life as a bachelor, the day you step into fatherhood, your old way of life ends, and an entire new life opens up.

I had been waiting for this moment my whole life. I wanted to start a family ever since I married my lovely wife Chandra. I knew from day one that she would make an amazing wife and loving mother.

Nevertheless, the question still crept in. I started to seriously question how we were going to survive, financially. As I struggled with these questions, I found myself on a new journey of deeper self-discovery.

That was when I realized the first major lesson: **Know Yourself.**

For some, it works perfectly to go all in and chase down goals in order to build our dreams faster.

For me, though, financial security is a core value. As much as I have the urge to work like a madman to realize my professional dreams, I realize that I'm naturally hardwired to relax—to be calm, cool, and collected. Deep down, I prefer to build on my dreams slowly, one brick at a time. It's more important for me to play it safe in order to keep food on the table, keep my wife happy, and provide for my daughter's needs.

My own life coach Terry King helped me reunite to my true values. In doing so, I realized that as much as I may not have liked it, my job allowed me the opportunity to become a father, to become the man searching for a house, to be the guy who spends time with his wife, time with his friends.

The second lesson on fatherhood took a little more time to learn: **You only have two choices in everything you do.**

You can either resent it for what it takes away from you or praise it for everything it allows you the opportunity to do.

The choice is yours to make.

Realize your perspective is yours to hold and can always be reframed. While what you have now may not seem the most appealing, it may be the one thing that's getting you closer to your dream, although you may not realize it at the time. The job you have may be the small stepping-stone to get you to the next level.

That next level may not land you your dream job, but it may provide a way for you to pursue your dreams in your spare time. It could provide the freedom to spend more time with your family, or the money to buy a house.

That next level could help you become the father you've always wanted to be. So praise the moment you're in. Praising beauty in the things you have continues to take you one step closer to the next level. Gratitude always moves you faster.

Always know your values, know what you are risking and what you're not willing to risk.

Above all, remember that as a father, you've accepted a new role in life. You're the leader of your home with a wife and a child to protect. It's time to go all in for your family.

Conversation Starter #1

What was your reaction when you first discovered you were going to be a father? Were you scared? Afraid you weren't equipped for the new job? The truth is that you are magnificent and worthy of this gift. Are there lies you need to quit telling yourself?

_____

_____

_____

_____

_____

_____

_____

_____

_____

_____

_____

_____

_____

_____

Conversation Starter #2

When have you felt that urge to quit, to go all in and jump for your dream? Did you stay or did you go? What was the deep-rooted reason you made the choice you did? Are you happy today with the choice you made?

_____

_____

_____

_____

_____

_____

_____

_____

_____

_____

_____

_____

_____

_____

_____

_____

Conversation Starter #3

Are you able to effectively balance finding your purpose and providing for your family? Do you know your core values? If not, how can you begin that journey of discovery?

_____

_____

_____

_____

_____

_____

_____

_____

_____

_____

_____

_____

_____

_____

_____

_____

Conversation Starter #4

Look at everything you have in your life as a father. Are you praising it for what it gives you or hating it for what it takes away? Why? How can you be grateful for your life as it is now?

_____

_____

_____

_____

_____

_____

_____

_____

_____

_____

_____

_____

_____

_____

_____

_____

Stay Connected/ Stay Dad

by Tommy Maloney

I love every minute of fatherhood, staying up all night, changing nappies, kids crying, I find it really funny and inspiring. It connects you to the world in a new way.

—Elton John

I think like any marriage, especially when you've had divorced parents like myself; you want to try even harder to make it work.

—Princess Diana

I did not want to be a dad.

Yes, I actually said that. And when I first got married, I negotiated with my then-wife that we only have one child. You see, when I was a kid, my parents divorced, so I did not want to bring a child into this world and end up being an every-other-weekend dad.

Well, spoiler alert. As soon as I found out I was going to be a dad, I became *that goofy guy*, talking to my wife's pregnant tummy. I guess deep down I did want to be a dad.

Everything was going well with the pregnancy until the checkup. The appointment was supposed to be routine. But the examining doctor announced that our baby was not going to form properly and we needed to move forward with an abortion.

Shock doesn't begin to describe my feelings at that moment. We walked out of the building, hugged, and went back to work. Once I got there, I walked into the office of the HR manager, shut her door, and cried.

A New Life, A New Dad

On March 11, 2003, at 5:04 am, Connor George Maloney was born. I was a dad! I was not only a dad but accepted the best job at the same time as a stay-at-home dad. Talk about on-the-job training! Sure, the pay was awful, but the benefits were outstanding. I got to see Connor's world every day and I loved it.

I was told that I would not be a good stay-at-home dad because I had never been a babysitter and because I was an only child and would not know what to do. Who said those things? Unfortunately, it was Connor's mom.

It was fuel for me to prove her wrong. As my relationship with Connor continued to grow, my wife began to resent my relationship with Connor. She felt that he and I created our own secret language—and we did. It was called father-son bonding.

As you might have guessed, the marriage did not last.

I made a promise to myself, though, that I would never be an absentee dad. I was going to be involved in Connor's life no matter what it took. I was not perfect, but I made it to his school events and had lunch at school with him. Connor was my good luck charm when the adult ice hockey team I played for won the championship.

I had been wrong all those years ago. I love being a dad.

A New Family

In 2010, I attended a fatherhood event in Denver, Colorado, run by a group of organizations working to promote positive fatherhood awareness. This was where I met Ann. At that time, I was working as a speaker, talking to others about being a divorced dad and helping men stay connected with their kids after a divorce or separation.

I had a speaking event before this particular meeting, so I was wearing a suit and one of my special ties that had pictures of Connor on it. Ann came up to me to say she really loved my tie. A month later, I was asked to speak at this organization's yearly meeting. After that, I received an email from Ann, letting me know that she really enjoyed my talk and wanted to know if we could go and get coffee.

On August 5, 2012, Ann and I were married. I went from being a dad with a son to what we call in our family a "bonus" dad with two bonus daughters, Betsy, who is 18, and Becca, who is 13. My son, daughters, Ann, and I are like *The Brady Bunch* (minus Alice). Raising girls is WAY different than raising boys, and if you have both, I am sure you're well aware of that. I am still learning how to handle things when one of the girls starts crying.

One thing's for sure. If you are raising daughters, you really need to have more patience than when you're raising boys.

My point of view is a bit unique because I have been in the girls' lives for only four years, but I feel I can connect first-time dads with newborns to bonus dads in a new relationship. When I first came into the girls' world—and especially when I moved in—I did not demand that it was my way or the highway. I needed to earn their respect first. Again, as a new dad, you need patience. As the bonus dad, you need to know where your place in the family is as far as the hierarchy goes.

In other words, it helps to leave your ego in a box. It's not about you; rather, it's about your kids. It's not about you, but about letting your partner know that she is amazing. I attend the girls' events, and I know my place. I am in the background; however, I show them I love them by supporting them when it comes to their time. I am present but, at the same time, I show respect to their birth dad by not making a scene.

Betsy

Betsy and I have our moments. She is going off to college this fall, so our relationship is like that of

35

housemates. I stay out of her way. I'm not saying that we can't be in the same room. I'm just saying I did not insist on the "my-house-my-rules" approach. I wanted us to develop a friendship.

When I was getting ready to propose to her mom, Betsy and I went out for coffee because I wanted to ask permission from her as well as Ann's parents. This is what I meant earlier about showing support, and the way I did it was by getting Betsy's permission and showing I wanted to be in her life and be there when she needed help.

When Betsy got her current car, she asked me to teach her how to drive a stick shift. When your kids can ask you to help them with a life event like that, it is a wonderful feeling. Yes, there are still times I feel that she and I just don't connect. But that's normal. It just goes back to having patience.

Becca

Becca is all heart. When Ann and I first got the kids together to see if we were going to continue the relationship, Becca was constantly asking me when I was going to marry her mom. Ann and I made a pact that if the kids didn't get along with each other, we were not going to continue and would move on, but things do happen for a reason.

The kids all get along like they truly are brother and sisters.

Becca is a wonderful kid. She sings, does gymnastics, and wears her big heart on her sleeve. Her birth dad treats her very differently than her older sister, and I feel bad for Becca. That is why she and I have such a tight bond. She and I have a fun and loving father–daughter relationship that I hope you have as well. (I will admit that last summer I paid her to clean up the dead snake we found in the front of the house. She is fearless.)

I am very blessed to have two daughters who are super smart and love Connor. I could not have asked to be placed in a better situation than I am in now. Raising girls is so different. I asked my father-in-law if it was me or if it really was different raising boys versus raising girls. He assured me it is much different.

I will repeat: the best advice I can give you if you have daughters is simply to have patience. But no matter if you have boys, girls, or both, you also need to TELL them you love them. You also need to let them learn from their mistakes. Realistically, I am not raising girls; they are raising me.

They push my buttons (yes, Connor does also) but I try to just be the best dad I can be. I screw up all the time, being a dad. But being part of our kids' lives is more important than any mistakes we make along the way. We are raising our kids to be better citizens, wives, mothers, husbands, and fathers.

My parents divorced when I was 5 years old, the same age Connor was when I was going through my divorce. The best thing about my own divorce was it gave me the opportunity to marry my soul mate and learn what it was like to raise girls. Connor might not get it, but the girls are raising him, too, and helping him learn how to treat a girl. If he doesn't, then his sisters just might take him on. Did I mention I love being a dad as well as a bonus dad?

Tommy is first and foremost a dad to his son Connor and his bonus daughters Betsy and Becca. Secondly he is the author of the book 25 Tips for Divorced Dads: How to create special memories and grow your bonds with your children. *He has been a keynote speaker for Colorado Fatherhood Convention and Every Thing For Dads. Tommy has spoken at Ignite 17 Fort Collins and is a TEDx speaker.*

For more information or to contact Tommy please go to blendingthefamily.com where you can sign up for his newsletter or subscribe to the podcast.

Conversation Starter #1

Did you want to be a dad when you first found out? Be honest with yourself. If you didn't want to be a dad, what have you done to change your mind?

Conversation Starter #2

What makes you the best dad you know? How do you ensure you won't be an absentee father? Was your father there for you?

_____

_____

_____

_____

_____

_____

_____

_____

_____

_____

_____

_____

_____

_____

_____

_____

Conversation Starter #3

How have you earned the trust of your daughter?
What does "trust" mean to you and your family?

_____

_____

_____

_____

_____

_____

_____

_____

_____

_____

_____

_____

_____

_____

_____

_____

Conversation Starter #4

Is your daughter raising you? What has she taught you thus far about women?

_____

_____

_____

_____

_____

_____

_____

_____

_____

_____

_____

_____

_____

_____

_____

_____

_____

Daddy-Daughter Weekends

by James Woosley

There's something like a line of gold thread running through a man's words when he talks to his daughter, and gradually over the years it gets to be long enough for you to pick up in your hands and weave into a cloth that feels like love itself.

—**John Gregory Brown,**
Decorations in a Ruined Cemetery

*To a father growing old
nothing is dearer than a daughter.*

—**Euripides**

We are fast approaching a time when, at least in the First World, it will become standard practice to select the gender of your children before you even get pregnant. That is a fascinating and scary thing to me.

My wife Heather told me she was pregnant in January of 2000. There are at least three reasons we got pregnant at that time: we stopped trying to get pregnant, I purchased a new used car for my birthday, and God has a sense of humor. Giving up and taking on debt may be a pretty good formula for having a first kid!

Heather and I have different philosophies on life (opposites attract, right?). As we approached ultrasound time, she wanted to know the gender of our new baby, and I wanted to be surprised in September. I thought it would add some excitement while she wanted to buy everything in pink or blue as soon as possible.

Knowing that staying married meant she would have to win, and that if she found out and I didn't, I'd soon figure it out, I gave in and accepted the early news.

I am the oldest child in my family. It was my worldview for how families are best structured. Son first, then daughter, then whatever comes next if you have more kids (this is where I know God is laughing at my 26-year-old self). When the ultrasound results came in and we found out we were having a daughter, I felt disappointed—for about a second. Then the phrase "daddy's little girl" popped in my head and I was in tears. This would be awesome!

A few months later we got the surprise and excitement I wanted, just not in the way I wanted to get it. Heather wasn't feeling well. An ER visit diagnosed severe preeclampsia. She had gained a significant amount of fluid weight in just a few weeks, and by July she was in the hospital.

I was clueless. She was a nurse, and I was an oblivious first-time father. My wife and daughter were in danger and there was nothing I could do about it.

On a stormy night in Omaha on July 11, 2000, my daughter Anna was born via emergency C-section. The pregnancy had lasted 27 weeks, and Anna weighed just 2.06 pounds (when .06 pounds is 3% of your body weight, it's worth noting).

She would spend more than two months in the Neonatal Intensive Care Unit and I would learn more about baby medicine and nursing than I ever wanted to know.

It was a horrible and wonderful time with many ups and downs. Heather struggled to recover as well, and I was doing anything I could to help them both. There isn't much training for becoming a new dad even when everyone is healthy. I'm thankful for the help of our families and that the same God who laughed at me held us in His hands throughout the ordeal.

Heather and Anna got better in the following months. The experience accelerated my departure from the United States Air Force, and within a year we were living in Alabama near Heather's family while I traveled 50 weeks a year as a technology consultant.

I was on the road pretty much every week for the next five years. In that time, we experienced an ectopic pregnancy and decided to adopt instead of risking Heather's health any further. (And God laughed once again when we tried to adopt a girl and ended up with a boy. Ian is another story for another book!).

My constant travel for work created some issues with family dynamics, but we found ways to make it work. When I came home and didn't leave, that created different dynamics and it took time to adjust.

After reading *Strong Fathers, Strong Daughters* by Dr. Meg Meeker, I got the idea to start taking Anna on an annual trip we call our Daddy–Daughter Weekend. Our first weekend was in 2009. We drove five hours from our home in Alabama to Atlanta. I think we were both a little nervous about it, but we were up for the adventure.

We stayed at a hotel (a big deal when you're nine years old), went swimming, and visited the World of Coca-Cola, Zoo Atlanta, the Georgia Aquarium, and the Fernbank Museum of Natural History. It was an exhausting, whirlwind trip crammed into about 36 hours, but it was a blast.

It was on that trip when I remember looking at my little girl and seeing a glimpse of the young woman she was becoming. She was still a kid, but growing up fast. I was a bit sad, but also encouraged.

We haven't been able to do a big trip every year, but since that first weekend in Atlanta, we've explored New Orleans, saw Fall Out Boy and Paramore in Tampa, and attended a Dan Miller seminar in Franklin, Tennessee. Last year we made a special trip back to Franklin for Anna to record some songs in a professional studio (she has real talent according to her biased father).

We also hang out a lot. We go out to movies and dinner dates and other events. I firmly believe that these intentional investments in father–daughter time are why we have a close relationship now that she's almost 16 years old (and it keeps us close even through normal teenage drama).

But the last seven years haven't been easy. Growing up can be hard. Anna has experienced significant health issues, some of which she will live with the rest of her life. She has had to grow up too fast at times.

I wish we had started the trips sooner and could do them with greater consistency. We often talk about possible future trips, dreaming of Colorado or New York City (or anywhere she can see some band she likes that makes me cringe).

One day she will go off to live her life, likely getting married and having children of her own. But my hope is that no matter what our lives are like, we can still find a way to have an annual Daddy–Daughter Weekend.

I challenge you to make a similar investment. Time together is more important than where you go, what you do, or how much you spend. Make the time to build deep connection as early as possible.

Don't do it to check off a box—do it because you love her and want her to know you love her.

Invest in one-on-one time with all of your kids. Boys are different than girls and the activities may or may not be the same, but it doesn't matter.

Be present, listen and laugh, and let them know you love them. In other words, just be Dad.

James Woosley is an underachiever—only because he's constantly expanding his potential by doing something amazing then immediately striving for more—knowing that his mind, body, and spirit have been stretched to a new level of possibilities.

As a publisher, business coach, and project manager, James helps people and organizations move ideas from the dreaming and planning stages to full implementation. He sets goals, plans strategically, and makes things happen...for himself and those around him.

He is the author of Challenge Accepted! *and* Conquer the Entrepreneur's Kryptonite.

Beyond serving his business clients, writing and publishing books, sitting on the board of education in his hometown and on the Executive Committee for the state school board association, James is a dedicated husband to his high school sweetheart, Heather, and a doting father to his children, Anna and Ian.

Connect with James online at JamesWoosley.com.

Conversation Starter #1

Have you ever documented the story of your daughter's birth? If not, take a moment to write down what happened. Include what you were thinking and feeling throughout that time.

_____

_____

_____

_____

_____

_____

_____

_____

_____

_____

_____

_____

_____

_____

_____

_____

Conversation Starter #2

Does the idea of a weekend alone with your daughter frighten or excite you? Maybe a little of both? What would be the ideal outcome from time alone together? How would it make your wife feel?

_____

_____

_____

_____

_____

_____

_____

_____

_____

_____

_____

_____

_____

_____

_____

Conversation Starter #3

Imagine some trips you and your daughter could take that would be fun and give you time to connect at a deeper level. Ask her what she thinks of the idea and where she would like to go.

_____

_____

_____

_____

_____

_____

_____

_____

_____

_____

_____

_____

_____

_____

_____

_____

Conversation Starter #4

Maybe a big trip isn't possible right now, and even if it is, one big trip won't be enough. You need to connect with your daughter as often as possible. Do you have any simple Daddy–Daughter date ideas?

_____

_____

_____

_____

_____

_____

_____

_____

_____

_____

_____

_____

_____

_____

_____

Good to Be Needed

by Rob Azevedo

Dear Daddy, No matter where I go in life,
who I get married to, how much time I spend with guys,
how much I love my husband,
You'll always be my number one man.
Your little girl.

—Anonymous

A good father is one of the most unsung,
unpraised, unnoticed, and yet one of the
most valuable assets in our society.

—Billy Graham

My daughter is 13 now—nearly a woman—and I've heard the advice a hundred times over.

"You better get ready," people say. "You have no idea what's coming down the pike. She's not going to have time for you anymore."

This is what I hear—what I've been hearing for a couple of years now—through the unnerving whine of some chardonnay heads helping themselves to my collection of wines. They tell me that my baby, my precious, sweet-faced baby girl, will soon be shutting me down or, rather, out.

Hand to face, lifeless hugs, no more calls...expect it all, they say. I can't picture it. Yet, these people insist my time has come.

Tonight, the well-meaning guests in our home proclaim that she's heading off into the hinterlands, home of the great awakening, where the world is exposed, zits and all.

(This I remember from my own "coming of age" days. I admit, those were heinous times, being introduced to the real world. I didn't know who to trust in my own home, let alone a world of strangers offering new beginnings.)

Then someone starts railing on about how the many lies my daughter will endure and tragedies she will witness will either inspire her or break her spirit, not to mention that she'll be exposed to rampant disease, soul-killing technology, and dead-end career paths...

"Stop it!" I cry out at the merry marauders draining my kitchen supply of hard beverages. "You've sucked my spine dry! Now leave my home!"

They just continue to serve me bitter wine.

Years ago, I could at least walk the floors at night worrying about anything and everything, knowing all the while that my kids were sleeping upstairs.

It was a maddening cycle.

I roared out to the masses, "I worried because she needed me!" finger to chest, my tongue burning with vermouth. "And she'll always need me!"

Then I hear some louse saying under his breath as he slugs down another mouthful of cold beer, "*Needed* is the key word in that statement."

"Screw that!" I screamed, fists pounding down on the porcelain countertop.

Curse all you want, they say, but as your transparency deepens and your need to be needed becomes more fragmented, well, that will penetrate you in ways unknown. You'll find yourself reaching back to your own worst days as you stare, lonely, into a bathroom mirror, scrambling for your own innocence.

What innocence?

I hung my head and the cranked up crowd of winos became a blur. I focused instead on a sneaker mark left on the kitchen floor, the heavy bottle in my hand long gone empty. Damn kids. Love them.

And that's what frightens me. Thirteen years ago, I was a rank mess of selfishness, but my baby girl's birth vaporized that guy, for the most part. I finally had a reason to care, to focus on someone besides myself, for once.

I can't lose that. I won't lose that. That guy must not return.

I tapped out for five minutes, letting the soul-crushing crowd simmer as I made my way to the bathroom. I would not allow this negative talk to ruin my night or dictate my relationship with my daughter. What we have developed over the past 13 years isn't just the common bond. And it's not built off lore and tradition. It's the bond of all bonds. Fortified in unconditional love and openness.

So why now, at this middle hour, just as her rising sun begins to crown on the distant horizon, would she abandon me?

I began talking to myself in the bathroom mirror, conducting an interrogation that Mike Wallace would be proud of.

And why do you think that her teenage years will be just like yours?

Doesn't it work like that?

No, it's her life. Not yours.

Will she deny me?

No, you can be there for her whether she likes it or not.

Ah, with space agreed upon, of course.

Of course.

It's not all about cell phones, is it?

No, she's a little woman now with little woman thoughts and little woman distractions and little woman instincts.

Ah, I will share my own experiences as a teen with her. Sharing is good.

No! Don't do that! Burn your past! It's diseased!

I hear what you're saying now. Do the Costanza and go opposite.

Something like that.

Walking out of the bathroom, I was steady once again, ready to take on all the chardonnay heads and their dismal shots at love and fate. But the kitchen was now empty. All the pessimistic prowlers had gone home.

All except my rock, my wife, who was washing wine glasses at the kitchen sink.

"Where'd everyone go?" I asked her.

"Oh, Peg and Fred had to go home. Their daughter Jenny got in a fight with her boyfriend and was all upset. She has a biology test in the morning, too. I feel bad for that poor thing."

That's terrible.

"Oh, and Paul and Amy promised to have a Food TV marathon night with their daughter who's home on vacation from UNH. She's a junior now. Can you believe it?"

Who?

"Anyway, Barb and Herb are going to swing by in the morning to take that nasty couch out of the basement and give it to their daughter Erica because she just got a new apartment in the city. Guess Herb got her a job with the state, and she's getting back on her feet. Good for her."

No, good for them. Good for all of us. Good to be needed.

Rob Azevedo, 45 from Manchester, NH, is married with a 14-year-old daughter and 11-year-old son. Azevedo has been in the homecare industry for the last 16 years but moonlights as a music columnist for the Concord Monitor, a radio host at WNHN 94.7 FM out of Concord, NH, and hosts a monthly "Artist in the Round" series at New England College.

Conversation Starter #1

Do you ever hide the love you have for your daughter to impress your friends? Or do you always let your authentic love shine through? How do you show your love?

_____

_____

_____

_____

_____

_____

_____

_____

_____

_____

_____

_____

_____

_____

_____

Conversation Starter #2

When you became a father, what led you to make the changes needed to care about someone else more than yourself? Was it difficult to adjust to selflessness?

_____

_____

_____

_____

_____

_____

_____

_____

_____

_____

_____

_____

_____

_____

Conversation Starter #3

What will you do in your role as a father to keep your daughter forever close to you in those critical teenage years? Home is where the heart is. Will you still hold her heart? Will you still be needed?

_____

_____

_____

_____

_____

_____

_____

_____

_____

_____

_____

_____

_____

_____

_____

Conversation Starter #4

If your daughter's teenage years were like yours, would you be proud? What if her adulthood looks like yours in the mirror? Are you showing her today who you want her to be tomorrow?

_____

_____

_____

_____

_____

_____

_____

_____

_____

_____

_____

_____

_____

_____

_____

_____

Headbutts and Barbie Dolls

by Adam Wernecke

*He didn't tell me how to live;
he lived, and let me watch him do it.*
—Clarence Budington Kelland

*The last of human freedoms - the ability to chose one's
attitude in a given set of circumstances.*
—Viktor E. Frankl

Her name is Pepper-Sue; I first met her almost three years ago.

She is a huge jerk, a princess, a snuggler, a confidant, a thief, and a connoisseur of all things edible. Above everything, she is my daughter, my long-awaited fourth child, and owner of huge crazy hair.

How can I pass along all my knowledge to this little spitfire? Can I equip her to be a strong and independent woman? I can only give her advice to lead her to become like the strong women I have known in my life, to give her the qualities I feel sets these women apart from followers, and makes them strong, confident women.

Grow strong, Pepper-Sue. Eat graham crackers, ice cream, and cereal. Run with your legs, hug with your arms, and think with your head. Look up and dream of flying.

Play with GI Joes and Barbies, make a gun out of a stick, chase squirrels, and pick up bugs. Watch construction workers and ask why. Never stop asking questions. Learn something new every day. Never stop learning about the whole world. If you want to learn how to weld, learn how to weld. If you like sewing or painting, then dive in and learn how!

Wear the clothes you want to wear. Put solid shoes on your feet, practical pants on your legs, and never put yourself at a disadvantage for the pleasure of men. Learn how to throw a punch, and never be afraid of head-butting a jackass. You don't need makeup to make you pretty. Pierce your body and tattoo your skin on your terms. The world will never stop telling you how a woman is supposed to behave and what she is supposed to look like. Others will try to tell you what the norm is, what sexy is, what beauty is. Don't take it at face value. Even my advice should be tempered by the song of your heart.

Let your hair grow long, then cut it all off and let it grow again. Throw a ball, fix a bicycle, learn to sew, and learn to throw knives. Become a well-rounded person.

Live your life to please your God; use your gifts and talents to build up and encourage your fellow humans. Let anger pass, don't let it live in your heart. Learn to live according to the fruits of the spirit: love, joy, peace, patience, kindness, goodness, faithfulness, gentleness, self-control. You can never go wrong if you live with those traits as your guide. Love everyone. Put yourself in the shoes of others to understand their viewpoints.

Analyze your life daily. Stay away from addictions. They will rule your life and rob you of control.

When you fail, get up and get at it again. Your life will never go so far down that it cannot come back up again. Get help when you need it. Lean on good friends and family for strength when you can't stand alone.

Be better tomorrow than you were today.

Make art, listen to your heart, find what you love and become great at it.

Let your life ebb and flow, live each section of your life as best you can. Sometimes, the days will be dark. Sometimes they will be filled with love and joy. Hurt will come to your heart. Don't run from it, but don't hold onto it forever. Pain sharpens the times of happiness.

Find a mate who completes you. He's out there. You don't need to do anything special to attract him. Your souls will drift together without the help of fashion, makeup, or your hairstyle. Be best friends and share your hurt and joy and dreams. You should be his queen and he your king.

Realize that your relationship will require that you feed it with love every day. Realize you are different; you are special individuals who need each other. Hold hands, hug, and hold onto each other. Share your frustrations with love and swallow your pride.

With love and respect to the woman you will become,

— Dad

Adam Wernecke is an artist, stay-at-home dad, and connoisseur of electronic gadgets living in Bay City, Michigan. He is married with four children; Gabe, Josh, Martigan, and Pepper-Sue.

He has worked in graphic design since leaving the United States Air Force in 2006, and has been an artist since he could pick up a pen. You can peruse his gallery and grab a piece of colorful art at adamwerneckeart.com.

When he's not painting he loves to build things and work on do-it-yourself projects around the house. He also loves drinking beer, from the very cheap to the very expensive, and even reviews his findings from time to time.

Conversation Starter #1

Are you being strong enough today to shape your daughter into the confident, beautiful, and strong woman of God she was created to be?

_____

_____

_____

_____

_____

_____

_____

_____

_____

_____

_____

_____

_____

_____

_____

_____

Conversation Starter #2

What are you doing to help your daughter embrace her own identity and avoid falling victim to the standards the world has set for her? She deserves to remain special. Do you tell her everyday she is beautiful, loved, and respected?

_____

_____

_____

_____

_____

_____

_____

_____

_____

_____

_____

_____

_____

_____

Conversation Starter #3

What new, exciting, crazy interest has your daughter shown lately that you welcomed her to explore 100 percent? Or did you shut her down as many parents often do?

_____

_____

_____

_____

_____

_____

_____

_____

_____

_____

_____

_____

_____

_____

_____

_____

Conversation Starter #4

How are you helping, shaping, and guiding your daughter to listen to her heart? Do you sing its praises with her?

_____

_____

_____

_____

_____

_____

_____

_____

_____

_____

_____

_____

_____

_____

_____

Be the Change You Want to See

by Marcus Kusi

To be as good as our fathers we must be better, imitation is not discipleship.

—Wendell Phillips

Each person must live their life as a model for others.

—Rosa Parks

I have been married since 2010 and have two wonderful daughters. It has certainly not been an easy job. Being a father is one of the best things to have happened in my life. I never knew my father, but I never let that hinder me from trying to be the best dad I could be for my girls.

I will never forget the moment I saw my daughters for the first time. I was like, *wow, I am a daddy now. It's no longer going to be just about my awesome wife and me. My girls will be calling me daddy. We are going to be a family.*

Since the day I became a father, my life has changed for the better. Every time I do something, I now ponder what my actions are *saying,* and what example I am setting for my daughters.

There have certainly been ups and downs, days when I felt completely clueless, when I failed as a dad, and did not live up to my expectations of what a great dad should be. Of course, there have also been days—moments, really—when I felt like I was doing all the right things.

Seeing my daughter's smile, giggle, and laugh with me are the precious moments money cannot buy, and I cherish them dearly. It is amazing how everything that once seemed so important or fun changes once you become a father.

My daughters are barely five years of age, yet I already have a lot of favorite memories to share with them when they are older.

For example, we love to take walks. To be honest, I am not a big fan of playing in the snow. In fact, I dislike snow very much, even though I live in New England.

However, I love going for walks with my daughters and wife. Even during winter when snow is everywhere, we still manage to go for a short walk.

We usually walk for about one to two miles, depending on the route we take. During these walks, my daughters will play on the roadside, jump in water puddles, run for a little bit, and sometimes pick up small bugs.

I have grown accustomed to pushing my comfort level and doing things just to see them smile and hear them laugh. I never thought I would let someone paint my nails, or do my makeup, but that's what being a father to two girls has brought me to.

I just love seeing them so alert and happy, filled with joy and excitement about life.

I am not the perfect dad. I am still new to parenting and learning as I go.

If you just became a dad or just found out you are going to be a dad, I hope the following four lessons based on my experience will help you in many ways on your journey as a father. They are the lessons I have learned and practice every day:

Mom and Dad are on the Same Team

You have to be on the same page with the mother of your child or children. This is one of the things that's helped me the most on my journey. I know it may not be easy to do, but do your best to make it happen. The benefits are special.

Share the responsibilities with your wife, and decide what you'll each be responsible for, from the little things like who changes the diapers all the way to the bigger things like how you raise and discipline your children.

Changing diapers, especially the messy, stinky ones, is not fun. You have to do it for your baby, and knowing that the mother of your child will be taking turns with you makes it easier.

When you are on the same page with her, you will be able to communicate effectively about how to raise your child, how much you spend on items for your child, and how you discipline, instead of fighting over who changes the poopy diaper.

Patience

This is one of my strongest personality traits. I was very patient before my daughters arrived, but they have tested my patience in many ways. Some days, I feel my limits had been reached, and I've had to learn how to be more patient with my daughters.

You see, they do not understand any language and they cannot speak very well. They cannot communicate their thoughts to me and their brains are not fully developed, so they can't really control many of their impulses.

Patience has been a critical skill for my journey of fatherhood. Without patience, I will not be able to become the great dad I want to be for my daughters.

Develop this skill as early as possible. It's going to be vital when your kids get older.

Be Their Role Model

I mentioned before that I never knew my father. One thing that had a tremendous impact on my life while growing up was having role models to look up to and emulate. I saw the types of lives they led, the kind of impact they had in society, and how they treated other people.

Just observing them showed me why and how I could have a positive impact on society. It also allowed me to learn from their mistakes.

As a father, your children will be learning a ton about life from your actions, from eating to sleeping and everything in between. Your goal should be to become someone they will be proud to call 'daddy', someone they will not be shy to introduce their friends to, someone they will respect and feel thankful for.

Be Present

Fatherhood brings many experiences, and you should be present during those times. For example, I am guilty of checking emails while playing with my daughters, and it has not helped us at all.

As a result, I made the decision to put my cell phone away whenever I am spending time with them. To help me achieve this goal, I turn my phone off and place it on the counter so I do not have easy access to it.

Maybe it's not your cell phone that interferes with your relationship. Whatever it is, address it, and do your best to be present when you are with them.

Fatherhood isn't always an easy journey, but you can make it a journey filled with lots of great memories. The key is stay in a state of learning so you can become the best version of yourself.

Marcus Kusi is a dedicated husband and passionate father who loves spending time with his family. Together with his amazing wife, he helps newlyweds adjust to married life, inspires married couples to improve their marriage, and hosts the First Year Marriage Show podcast.

He co-authored Communication in Marriage: How to Communicate with Your Spouse Without Fighting *to help married couples communicate better.*

To connect with Marcus, visit ourpeacefulfamily.com.

Conversation Starter #1

Your wife is your biggest supporter and the one who will be there no matter the decisions you make. Are you respecting her values as you raise your daughter?

_____

_____

_____

_____

_____

_____

_____

_____

_____

_____

_____

_____

_____

_____

_____

_____

Conversation Starter #2

Patience is a virtue. If you don't have it yourself, how can you ever give it to your children? When have you lost patience with your daughter? What was it that had you so anxious? Relive that experience from her eyes, and ask what would have been different had you demonstrated patience?

_____

_____

_____

_____

_____

_____

_____

_____

_____

_____

_____

_____

_____

_____

Conversation Starter #3

Whether you know it or not, your daughter is looking at you as an example of who she should be. Are you proud of the role model you are giving her? What can you change today to improve the image of you that your daughter sees?

_____

_____

_____

_____

_____

_____

_____

_____

_____

_____

_____

_____

_____

_____

_____

Conversation Starter #4

Presence is the most difficult thing we can achieve, especially as fathers. What steps are you currently taking to obtain an increased presence in your daughter's life? Doesn't she deserve to have all of you when you're with her?

_____

_____

_____

_____

_____

_____

_____

_____

_____

_____

_____

_____

_____

_____

Sunday Somethings

by Sean Ackerman

co-authored by
Alexandria and Cassandra Ackerman

Dad—a son's first hero, a daughter's first love.

—Anonymous

As a new father, you only have two choices.
You can do what's right or what's responsible.
Choose wisely.

—Jason Pockrandt

As busy fathers, we all try to connect with our children. This is even truer of daughters. With my two daughters, (Ally, 12 and Cassie, 10) I found connection even more important because I don't share their gender. But what I lacked in estrogen, I made up for in experiences.

Growing up, my parents both worked, sometimes two jobs at a time. Time with them was very fleeting. When my wife and I were first married, we both worked exceptional hours. I didn't want to repeat history. Certain catalysts opened my eyes, and I realized that, as a father and husband, I owed my family and myself something more.

We made the decision that once we had children, we would scale back and work alternating shifts so that one of us was always spending time with the kids. Most of the time, my wife was with them during the days, and I was with them on nights and weekends.

This was when I realized it wasn't the money I spent on them, but the experiences that counted — that spending time with my children that was so valuable. With my wife working generally every Sunday, I was home alone with the girls for an entire day, at least until 5pm when my wife came home.

I began a process—I call it a process because I'm a productivity geek—of planning out my Sundays and planning out my activities with the kids so we could do something fun. I began what I now call *Sunday Somethings.*

One of the first Sunday Something adventures was taking my children, who were 4 and 6 at the time, to a paddle fest on the Hudson River. What did they know about kayaks? About as much as their old man did. But we walked around, talked to the vendors, and just had a good time.

From that first experience, Sunday Somethings evolved into many different things. We saw a lot of movies (one of my favorite pictures is the three of us wearing our Avengers T-shirts for the movie launch) and we explored other areas of the Hudson Valley where we lived.

I made them explore nature and hike local trails and visit museums and historic sites. They would say, "Boring," the whole ride there. But after ten minutes of trudging through the gardens of the Vanderbilt Mansion in Hyde Park, they would lose themselves in the views and the large fields to play in. By the end of the day, I would hear, "Let's go back there again."

I made them write stories about the favorite thing they did on their summer vacation. I wrote a story too. For young second and third graders, this was torture, but they wrote the stories and even illustrated them, and when we were done, we had three different stories on any one topic.

We would then stand up and act out the stories, voting at the end for the story we liked best and why. We clapped for each other, showing appreciation for the work the person had done, and each of us worked on our stage presence. The things that happened when we did this were amazing.

Here's an example of one of my stories:

> *"My favorite thing I did on my summer vacation was to go scuba diving. When my family went to Lake George, I went on the Mini-Ha-Ha and it sailed to the center of the lake. I suited up and jumped off the side of the boat. I saw a large creature at the bottom that looked like a dinosaur. When I went back to shore, I told them I had discovered the 'Lake George Monster.'"*

I made it simple to show my youngest how easy it was.

My 9-year-old daughter Ally wrote:

"I did a lot of things like sleep until 1pm [sorry to interject, but truly a proud parent moment here]. My favorite was when Harold gave me his purple crayon. I drew a lot of things and everything came to life. I drew a purple sports car and a purple cell phone. I made a box around Cassie [sisterly love] and she did the mime thing. It was fun."

Ally decorated the bottom half of the page with clouds and rain and all sorts of weather phenomenon.

My 8-year-old daughter Cassie wrote:

"This summer, I went on the Disney Cruise. I went on a zip line on the cruise. I went on the water slide. I went in the arcade and won a million tickets. I liked it because I did it by myself."

Short, sweet, and to the point. That's my Cassie. Some of our other story titles included:
- *Me and My Pet Walking*
- *A Day in the Woods*
- *My Pet Reindeer*

- *My Day with Santa Claus* [Holidays = Great Topics!]
- *In the Kid Cave I Painted!*
- *When My House Caught Fire!* [We had lost our house in a fire.]

Then I decided to get a little tricky and take a hint from the TV show *Chopped*, where they add in mystery ingredients. Ta-da—mystery words to make up a story with. Here are some of those hit titles:

- *Lamp, Salt, and Flower*
- *Green, Pot O Gold, and Magic*
- *One Direction, Flag and Tent Pole*

That particular idea died out after three tries, but we continued to crank out stories for the next year. One of my favorites was, *I Am Thankful For*.

Of course, I went first:

> *"I am thankful for my family. Coming from a small one, it really changed my life for the better to be surrounded by such a large, loving, and caring group of people. Through them, I have built relationships that will grow for the rest of my life. Those people, the ones I now call family,*

have touched my daughters' lives so much, and they are an inspiration to them as well. Giving, caring, loving, and helping are all things they do every day, and, in turn, these actions are reflected back to them from me."

Ally wrote:

"I am thankful for going on vacations. I like Disney because of the rides. I like Hershey because of the chocolate. I like NYC because of the buildings and stores. I like these places because I have a lot of fun on these vacations. I can't wait to go again."

And I'm okay with this, since her vacations are always spent with Mom and Dad.

Cassie wrote:

"I am thankful for school. School is fun and we play games too. I did Girls on the Run after school this year. I ran a 5K and it was fun. We get to do a lot of clubs in fourth grade. Fourth grade is really fun but it is my last year of COH [Cornwall on Hudson, her elementary school]."

This story ended with a frowny face, and it was nice that, even though she was sad, she could express herself.

We didn't write stories every weekend, but we wrote enough to capture the snapshots of their attitudes, likes, and dislikes. These moments in time are a peek into the world of their imagination. I created an experience, a memory, and a legacy that my girls will always remember.

The written stories were only a small part, and the performance and competition made for an entirely memorable experience. But the best part was that we shared something truly special.

If you get a chance and your children are into trying something new, give Sunday Somethings a try. It's a very simple process, and I guarantee you will reflect back on those times with your children. The stories were only one part of our Sundays, but we enjoyed going to fun places and having good times together.

As I mentioned in the beginning of this chapter, my children are now 10 and 12. I can look back and recall a multitude of experiences I had with them that my parents didn't have with me. I'm very proud of that as a father.

Thank goodness my wife worked on Sundays, because it allowed me to connect with these beautiful young girls and create many memories.

Sean Ackerman has been overcoming adversity since pre-conception. As his parents were told they would never have children, he fought his way into this world, bringing success in whatever he put his mind to. He's spent more than 25 years as a consultant, teacher and speaker for small privately-owned companies as well as large corporate organizations, including Columbia University, the New York State Police and Wal-Mart Stores..

In 2011, he and his family were left homeless after Hurricane Irene. Despite losing almost everything, they persevered to put their lives back together.

Today his show, You Leading You, shares insightful lessons from great leaders telling their stories of success. Sean also speaks and facilitates lessons on leadership with organizations and contributes to such influential platforms as The Huffington Post, The Good Men Project, Addicted 2 Success, *and others.*

Join Sean at youleadingyou.com for great self-leadership and inspirational content.

Conversation Starter #1

Sunday for many is a day of rest, but it can also be a day of family fun. Are you taking the time to be a father to your daughter and truly get connected after being gone at work all week? What will be your next Sunday Something?

_____

_____

_____

_____

_____

_____

_____

_____

_____

_____

_____

_____

_____

_____

_____

Conversation Starter #2

When we are raised without having shared experiences with our parents, it is imperative to break the cycle for our daughters. What is the ONE experience you never had with your parents that you'd like to share with your daughter now?

_____

_____

_____

_____

_____

_____

_____

_____

_____

_____

_____

_____

_____

_____

Conversation Starter #3

Are you taking enough creative time to devise new and exciting ways to share the world with your daughter when your spouse is away? Do you take her to the museum, parks, and activities? Or do you simply go where you want to go?

_____

_____

_____

_____

_____

_____

_____

_____

_____

_____

_____

_____

_____

_____

Conversation Starter #4

Too often, as new parents, we relive our childhood, good or bad, and pass that on to our children. You are not your parents and the story they lived. You are you. What will you commit to doing different today to ensure that you always stay true to yourself as a parent and don't fall into ways of parenting that hurt your heart?

_____

_____

_____

_____

_____

_____

_____

_____

_____

_____

_____

_____

_____

_____

A Father's Conversation: Advice to His Daughters

by John Wernecke

It was my father who taught me how to value myself. He told me that I was uncommonly beautiful and that I was the most precious thing in his life.

—Dawn French

Daughters of God: Know that you were formed by God's hands, dreamed up in His heart, and placed in this world for a purpose.

—Anonymous

Fatherhood is the most important role, vocation, or pursuit a man undertakes in his life, just as motherhood is to a woman.

As parents, you are the primary shapers of the character and values of your children. The people they become will affect society for years to come. Sometimes it's difficult to see that far ahead

Our challenge as dads is to prepare our children to see the value of each day as a step to the future. So the words I would like my daughter to hear with her heart are these:

It Takes Time to See a Better Way

Fathers are not born fully prepared for the task. Giving every important lesson for life to their children isn't easy.

My greatest mistake as a dad was being too focused on the future and trying to build something better for your future. By doing so, I messed up your todays. I was not living focused on the present, and I missed many little moments of engagement and connection each day.

My confession is that even though I am flawed and have not always practiced the things I speak of, they are still valuable lessons.

We are all learning. Adults may seem to have it all together, but the truth is they are learning as much about raising children as you are about life itself.

Honor Yourself

Honor yourself every day as a special, gifted, and valued person no matter what you may be feeling, no matter what others—enemies, even family, friends, and teachers—may say. We live in a culture that is very focused on the negative. It highlights what is wrong with our communities, relationships, families, etc.

This negativity has a way of soaking into our thinking. It tends to minimize or blur all the blessings in our lives, and even the good within ourselves. This is why it is vital that we intentionally see and hold onto what is good and positive.

We should intentionally seek out, look for, and celebrate with gratitude the good people, good smells, good sights, and good behaviors that are continually coming into our lives each day.

Recognize the Value of Authority

The writer of Proverbs 4:18, says, "But the path of the righteous is like the light of dawn, which shines brighter and brighter until full day." (As a small child, the authority of your parents protects you. When you listen and obey your parent as the authority, you will be protected.)

Parents and most adults have an advantage over children, because adults usually see the hazards and dangers that children can't see. This advantage comes with life experience and seeing life with a wider view. A wise, respectable child will grow to understand and respect their parents' authority as they mature. They will also learn that to earn the respect of others, they must show respect.

A great story that illustrates what happens when this kind of warning is misunderstood or disregarded can be found in "Genghis Khan and His Hawk," which can be found in the *Book of Virtues* by William J. Bennett. I would recommend reading this story—and the whole book—to your children when possible.

Learn the Value of Discernment

I have heard teenagers tell me about advice that

has been offered to them by their "friends." (Be careful about what you call something or someone).

The advice from their "friends" went something like this: "Smoking will help you calm down," or, "It's okay to skip school once in a while. Everyone does," or, "You can drive without insurance. It won't hurt anybody."

All of this advice overlooks the consequences of these actions. If we think there is no harm breaking these rules or laws, then we act according to such advice. However, listening to advice of "friends" like this will lead you to a false sense of security that, at some point, will collapse.

Discernment takes the time to ask if a friend's advice will cause harm. A genuine friend will not entice you away from goodness, honesty, and honoring genuine authorities.

Savor the Blessings of God

Realize that just by virtue of your birth and the care of your parents, family and friends—and even people you will never meet—you are protected, loved, fed, healthy, and talented.

The knowledge of these gifts and what you

do with them will determine their value to you. As you value them and use them, you will provide a heritage to your family and future generations.

I have benefited from a precious and helpful partner, teachers and many other people, as well as from books, houses, medicine, and other things that I didn't make myself or even understand. Yet, because of them, my life has been immeasurably blessed. I never want the smallest of gifts given to me or used by me to be taken for granted.

Don't Be Afraid to Make Mistakes

I added this because I believe it is very important to have an optimistic, positive view of failure.

For much of my life, I felt as if I were not good enough. I didn't really apply myself to study, reading, and learning. I saw others as being worth more, better, or more significant than I was because of my poor skills. This led to much self-criticism and negativity, which gripped my identity.

Reading about Thomas Edison, who is known for inventing the light bulb, gave me a new point of view. I don't know why I had never seen mistakes from this point of view before, but what I learned enlightened me. I learned not to feel bad about mistakes and failures because you can learn from them and eventually succeed.

Thomas Edison is said to have failed at least 1,000 times before succeeding in the invention of the light bulb. Now his invention is lighting up the planet.

The only person who is a failure is the one who doesn't keep trying. Remember, mistakes are part of how we learn, so risk failing and making mistakes, but always know you can get up, try again, and persevere. This is what truly defines your character.

These are just a few of the facts of life I would like you to know, to take to heart, and practice in your daily life. They are lessons I've learned from reading books, watching people, and observing behavior and its consequences.

I've tried to analyze, process and synthesize it all to find what's at the core. However, this is not the limit of wisdom or guidance I have to offer. There is more, and I am always ready to listen and work to bring the light of wisdom to the challenges of your life.

May God always guide you, walk with you, and lead you into the future with hope and courage.

Blessings, peace, joy, hope, and laughter,

— Your Dad

John Wernecke and his wife, Susan, live in Bay City, Michigan. He is a certified Laughter Yoga Leader, a retired Lutheran Pastor, and an incredible mentor to multitudes. His mission in life is to share the great news of positivity and joy while reminding us of the ultimate gift known as Baptism. You can read more at upwithpositivity.com.

Conversation Starter #1

Everything in life is good or bad based merely on our perspective. When have you taken a moment to look upon a bad situation and teach your daughter how to see the positive within the negative?

_____

_____

_____

_____

_____

_____

_____

_____

_____

_____

_____

_____

_____

_____

_____

_____

Conversation Starter #2

Failure happens, especially as a father raising daughters. When you last failed as a father, how did you feel? How did you respond? Are you able now to teach your daughter that failure is an illusion—only a lesson to be learned?

_____

_____

_____

_____

_____

_____

_____

_____

_____

_____

_____

_____

_____

_____

_____

_____

_____

Conversation Starter #3

What blessings in your life have you taken for granted lately? Is your daughter healthy, loving, clothed, protected, and fed? Cherish all you have today for what it gives you.

_____

_____

_____

_____

_____

_____

_____

_____

_____

_____

_____

_____

_____

_____

_____

_____

Conversation Starter #4

Practice discernment as a father and help your daughter to understand and use it when she is with her friends. How did you handle it the last time your daughter lacked discernment with a friend's advice?

_____

_____

_____

_____

_____

_____

_____

_____

_____

_____

_____

_____

_____

_____

The Protection of a Fatherless Father

by Josh Rivers

*I'm your father. It is my job to protect you.
It's a job I refuse to quit,
and at which I can't afford to fail.*

—Uncle Phil (*Fresh Prince of Bel-Air*)

*I cannot think of any need in childhood
as strong as the need for a father's protection.*

—Sigmund Freud

Fatherhood really changed my perception of life. I became a father at 25 when my son Joshua Jr. was born. It was a test of patience. For some reason, he missed all of the prerequisites for being a well-behaved child while he was in the womb. I (and his mother) had to start his training from the beginning.

He was stubborn and strong-willed. His love of adventure and absence of fear tested his mother and me regularly as he would wander off in public or run through the church naked during a funeral.

I was constantly working to make him tougher. Boys, after all, shouldn't cry. Disappointments happen, and he just needed to learn to deal with it like a man.

Then, there's my daughter, Abigail. She also didn't take any classes prior to birth, but we thought we were prepared after experiencing her big brother. However, we realized that she was different than our son. She wasn't quite as adventurous and was afraid of more things.

I also realized that trying to make her tough like a man didn't work well. I had to learn that she didn't always need to be told to stop crying, or to suck it up or be a man. Telling her that she cried like a girl was a compliment, not a put down to stop crying. It didn't take long to realize I was the one who needed to change.

I spent my life hiding my feelings. No crying. No emotion. It was usually hard for people to tell if I was happy or excited, or if I was sad or upset.

I never really knew my dad growing up, and I don't remember showing or feeling emotion either way about him. I'm not exactly sure why I always felt this way—maybe it was the responsibility I felt as the oldest child—but I always felt I had to be strong for my brother, sister, and mom.

My daughter helped me to see that I needed to show more compassion, even when she does something stupid and gets hurt. I needed to learn to spend a lot more time cuddling and comforting her.

It seemed so foreign to me. I had to learn how to get myself from an emotionless state to where she needed me to be.

I started to realize that one of the reasons I do what I do is because of my desire to protect. I wanted to protect my siblings growing up (even though they conspired to get me in trouble). I wanted to protect my mom. When I got married, I wanted to protect my wife. Then I wanted to protect my kids.

Protection is great, but there are different ways to provide it. There's the hide/restrain method I had been trying. There's a place for that, sometimes. But there's another way.

One of the things I want to protect my daughter from is dating the wrong guy. It may be 15 years down the road, but I still worry about it. I could approach it the tough-guy way and set rules and regulations and force her to only see people I approve of. This, by itself, can cause friction, rebellion, and regret.

A better, deeper, and longer-lasting way to do it is to set the example. If I want her to only spend time with guys who will really respect her, treat her right, and border on worshipping her, the best thing I can do is to do those things myself. I need to treat her like the princess she is. I need to open doors for her; compliment her; show compassion and sympathy; and respect her space, needs, and privacy.

Rules need to be set, and I should watch who she is around because in her youth she will be ignorant of many things. She won't always see bad character. But if I teach her, through example, what a good man should be like, it will make the job much easier for both of us.

I'll be teaching her what to expect from a man, and not to accept anything less. If she meets a guy and he doesn't do those things for her, she'll be the one who will want to break it off and I won't necessarily have to. When I do have to step in, she'll know from years of experience that I really do have her best interests in mind.

I can accomplish my goal of protection while still providing it in the way she needs and responds to it best. I can love her through protection without hiding her in the shadows of my own walls.

Josh Rivers became a Christian in 1998, a husband in 2003, and a father in 2006. Each of these new roles revealed a new set of character traits that needed improvements.

Josh is also a podcaster. Since 2013, he has hosted several shows and published hundreds of episodes. His skills led him to help others with their podcasts. He formed his business as Podcast Guy Media, LLC, in early 2016. With a goal of replacing his full-time factory job with this new business, he strives to spend time with his family as well.

Find out more and connect with Josh at joshuarivers.net or podcastguymedia.com.

Conversation Starter #1

Be honest. Have you ever told your daughter to stop crying. It's time to embrace your emotions as a man and a father. Are you being vulnerable enough around your daughter to show her she can do the same?

_____

_____

_____

_____

_____

_____

_____

_____

_____

_____

_____

_____

_____

_____

_____

Conversation Starter #2

How do you protect your daughter without becoming overprotective? When you're overprotective, you run the risk of pushing her further away. Are you restraining her and calling it protection because of your own upbringing?

_____

_____

_____

_____

_____

_____

_____

_____

_____

_____

_____

_____

_____

_____

_____

Conversation Starter #3

What will it take for you to shift from the hide/restrain method of fatherhood to a caring, loving, demonstrating model? Will it be challenging for you to release some of the control over who your daughter sees? Why?

_____

_____

_____

_____

_____

_____

_____

_____

_____

_____

_____

_____

_____

_____

_____

_____

Conversation Starter #4

As a father and husband it is our role to protect our wife and daughter. How do you define protection?

_____

_____

_____

_____

_____

_____

_____

_____

_____

_____

_____

_____

_____

_____

_____

_____

If You Have Bread on the Table, Then You're a Bread Winner

by Greg Gamache

When I was a boy of 14, my father was so ignorant I could hardly stand to have the old man around. But when I got to be 21, I was astonished at how much the old man had learned in seven years.

—Mark Twain

Change who you are. Become who you want to be.

—Jason Pockrandt

As a father to a daughter and stepdaughter, I have my hands full in raising up honorable women of God.

One of the most significant roles I have taken on in my new marriage was to become the father that my new wife's children didn't have. I had to overcome the hurdle of entering a new blended family and earn the trust and respect of my new daughter.

Here are some of the things I learned on how to earn the love and respect of daughters:

Become a Foundational Man

First, I decided that second to my relationship with God, I wanted my relationship with my wife to be the single strongest relationship I had, and I wanted to be the husband my wife wanted to have.

I was 40 years old when I married my wife. I admit that I had some old baggage I had to drop and a lot of old ways to unlearn in order to become the man I wanted to be.

We always question ourselves: *Am I going the right way; am I doing the right thing? Am I measuring up to my contemporaries?* We always want to be accepted and feel like we belong.

Men are all born with insecurity that can only be cured by having a strong relationship with God the Father.

A Man Must Become Decisive

He needs to be sure of the path he is following and the choices that he is making. It is the role for the man to be the head of household. To do so effectively, he must feel secure in the destiny he is striving for.

Make sure the course you are following is the proper course, and be strong enough to get that message across to your wife, who is the one you're leading.

Love and Respect in Marriage

As described by Emerson Eggerichs in his book *Love and Respect*, women are prewired to love and it is not difficult for a woman to love. They do not have to work toward it. Men find it easy to respect other men, whether they have a PhD or a GED.

Herein lays the problem for many men that radiates onto their daughters and must be corrected immediately for the family unit to succeed.

Men are to love their wives, and wives are to respect their love. The wife needs to be loved and the husband needs to be respected.

The "crazy cycle" of lack of love and respect stops when someone says, "Wait, this has to stop."

There is a conscious choice that is made for the man and women to love each other. When both parents make the conscious choice to love each other, they radiate those good vibes of commitment to the children in their home.

How often do you love your wife and demonstrate that love for her in front of your daughters? Love your wife and demonstrate that love openly in front of the children.

When you can give that love and respect to your children, you can help your daughters to flourish in their lives. You are giving your girls the most important things they will ever need in their lives.

Children Need Both Love and Respect

They are special to you. It's your job to affirm their beauty, value, and importance on a regular basis from an early age.

If your daughter comes to you and asks if

you can talk, she is telling you that she loves you and trusts what you have to say. She is being open to what you have to share, and that is a powerful moment in your relationship. Let your daughter know, feel, and see that she is accepted and belongs.

"Train up a child in the way that they should go, and when they are old, they will not depart from it"

—Proverbs 22:6

Behavior is Caught, Not Taught

If you make a promise to your daughter, keep your word. If you tell her in the morning you will play catch with her when you get home, play catch when you get home. Follow through.

When given the opportunity, you have the chance to build trust and demonstrate what integrity looks like.

If you drop the ball enough, your daughter will stop asking. If you continue this way, your daughter will begin to settle for less because she will come to believe she's not worth more.

The example you set as a man is the expectation of men you set for your daughter. They will believe that what you show is what they should expect from men, and they will find a low-life they can just settle for. They lower their own standards. I taught my children to never settle for anything in life.

Girls marry their fathers, meaning they are attracted to men who are like their fathers.

The most important thing that a man can do for his daughter is to give her genuine love and attention. Give her your full, undivided attention. Then she will marry a man who genuinely loves her.

Here are some final words of wisdom about raising girls that my father taught me at a young age. I embraced the lesson, carried it forever, and never let it go until I passed it onto my ladies:

There is nothing that you can't do and nothing that you can't be. However, know that if you're going to make that choice to do it, you better jump in with both feet.

You don't have to make a million dollars to be a breadwinner. You don't have to make $50,000 to be a breadwinner. As long as there is bread on the table, you're a breadwinner.

Greg Gamache is a retired father of five and grandfather of four. During his life he has been a musician, pastor, Bible teacher, and held many management positions in various corporations. Greg lives with his wife in Rockford, Michigan, and looks forward to spending time with their grandchildren.

Conversation Starter #1

Becoming a foundational father begins with laying the foundation in your home and marriage. Are you putting in an adequate amount of love and support for your wife to demonstrate that bond for your daughters?

_____

_____

_____

_____

_____

_____

_____

_____

_____

_____

_____

_____

_____

_____

Conversation Starter #2

Are you stuck on the feeling that you are not providing enough for your family and daughter? Know that you are a breadwinner. How can you believe more in yourself and show that belief to your daughter?

_____

_____

_____

_____

_____

_____

_____

_____

_____

_____

_____

_____

_____

_____

Conversation Starter #3

Be decisive on your journey and make that clear to the ones you're leading (wife and daughter.) Are you decisive enough on your path to teach your daughter how to find and follow her own path?

_____

_____

_____

_____

_____

_____

_____

_____

_____

_____

_____

_____

_____

_____

_____

_____

Conversation Starter #4

Can you recall the last time your daughter said, "Dad, can we talk?" If you can't, or if it's been too long, it's time to re-engage with the relationship. She needs you. She trusts you. Go help her.

_____

_____

_____

_____

_____

_____

_____

_____

_____

_____

_____

_____

_____

_____

_____

_____

Daddy, Can I Marry You?

by Desmond Bibbs

Fathers: Be your daughter's first love. Open doors for her, pull out her seat, talk to her, and treat her with the utmost respect. Set expectations on how a man should treat a lady and she will never settle for anything less.

—Anonymous

I am not ashamed to say that no man I ever met was my father's equal, and I never loved any other man as much.

—Hedy Lamarr

Until you are given the responsibility of raising a daughter, you don't realize the true worth of a woman. As a father, you fear for the mental and physical well-being of your daughter and act on the natural instinct to protect her from all the dangers this world makes her vulnerable to.

My experiences are teaching me that, as much as I desire to, I can't protect her from the woes of the world. Thus, my best defense is to properly equip her for the real obstacles life will present her with.

The influence I have over my beautiful 6-year-old daughter Destiny immediately hit me one day when she was observing me showing my wife the affection of a hug and a kiss. She looked and, after a brief moment of silence, she asked, "Daddy, can I marry you?"

Awed by such a question, I knew my response had to be intentional. I responded, "Absolutely!"

I understood, in that moment, she was telling me that she desired to marry a man like her father. It only makes sense, seeing that I am the most influential male figure she sees daily.

That question forced me to revisit my entire relationship with not only her, but with my wife and Destiny's brothers.

As I reflected more on this, I started to evaluate other relationships I could identify with.

I know an individual who as a child watched her father abuse her mother, and, as a result, she pursued relationship after relationship that included domestic violence.

I know an individual who never knew her father and, as a result, sought validation from men she pursued, thinking that using her body as a tool would translate to committed relationships.

Amongst other examples, it was clear to me the importance of my role as a father because my daughter will marry a man with the characteristics that I demonstrate to her.

So, at this point, my options are clear and concise:

1) Give in to the natural instinct to protect her at all costs by sheltering her from the woes of the world, or

2) Be the man I desire for her to spend her life with by setting a healthy and consistent example of what a good relationship looks like. Then I must trust and support the decisions she makes and have

faith that I have invested enough into her to be successful.

I choose the later, and I would encourage you to do the same.

Desmond Bibbs is a husband, father, and community leader, involved with Junior Achievement, READ Program, Bay City Chamber of Commerce, and Just for Kids. He is the owner of All Night Affairs. He also serves as a youth leader at his church. He and his wife, Shontaye, have three children: Brennan, Destiny, and De'Shon.

Conversation Starter #1

Have you invested enough in your daughter's life for her to be successful without the protection of her father? Have you been overprotective without realizing it?

_____

_____

_____

_____

_____

_____

_____

_____

_____

_____

_____

_____

_____

_____

_____

_____

Conversation Starter #2

What is the biggest fear you hold for your daughter? How are you going to move past that fear today?

_____

_____

_____

_____

_____

_____

_____

_____

_____

_____

_____

_____

_____

_____

_____

_____

Conversation Starter #3

How can you be more intentional with the responses you give to your daughter? Do you stop to think before you speak, sharing wisdom rather than reactionary answers?

_____

_____

_____

_____

_____

_____

_____

_____

_____

_____

_____

_____

_____

_____

Conversation Starter #4

How would you answer today if your daughter asked, "Daddy, can I marry you?"

_____

_____

_____

_____

_____

_____

_____

_____

_____

_____

_____

_____

_____

_____

_____

_____

Conclusion:
Daddy, Where
Are You Going?

by Jason Pockrandt

This is the price you pay for having a great father. You get the wonder, the joy, the tender moments - and you get the tears at the end, too.

—Harlan Coben

Live as if you were living a second time, and as though you had acted wrongly the first time.

—Viktor E. Frankl

I hope that you found this book helpful in your own journey through fatherhood. I have pulled together ten of the best and brightest fathers I know to give you a look into their lives, to learn from their mistakes, and to aspire to their levels of greatness as fathers.

I think that's what dads really want: to be the greatest person our daughter has ever known, and to be the coolest, smartest, kindest, and most courageous man in her life. The one she will always look up to and respect. The man she turns to for all the answers, even, at times, after she's married.

As a young millennial father, I know this journey is for the rest of my life, and I get to make it with my beautiful wife Chandra and our daughter Lenox. I couldn't ask for anything better.

I know who and what matters most in my life, and I understand becoming a great father won't happen automatically. I cannot wake up one day and be the center of my daughter's heart without being intentional. I have to do the work to become the father that she needs. The father she deserves.

Doesn't your daughter deserve better than what you had to experience? You may interpret *better* however you'd like. I know what life looked like for me, when I lost my Dad. I had 17 years with my father, and, while they were not all the best, they were still the ones I had. I cherish every moment that I was given with him, but had no clue that he would be gone from me so soon.

Do you ever take a moment to cherish the fact that you are here? You are given one more day to be a dad, to make a difference, to watch your daughter smile when she looks into your eyes. These are the moments and the days that matter most. These are the legacies we leave behind. We must make the time and take the first step to have our own *Father–Daughter Conversations.*

As fathers, we tend to continually judge ourselves for our lack of success at each level of our lives when we're not where we think we should be or we're not earning enough money to provide.

We have talked a lot in this book about what it means to be a real man and being able to share your emotions with your daughter. When you are given the chance to show your true self and to let your feelings out, embrace it for all that it's worth. Those moments bring out the best in us. There will be plenty of other times for you to be a strong man and to protect your daughter. Know the difference and be able to use discernment when you balance these two roles.

As Greg Gamache says, "Strength does not mean being stoic, and having emotion does not mean being weak and wimpy."

Become the husband you were created to be and live the life of the father that you've always dreamed you would be.

Acknowledgements

To my amazing wife Chandra: you're the reason this book exists. Without your love there would be no buggy boo and I would not be a father.

You're my rock and my foundation in my life as husband and entrepreneur. I can't imagine anyone else next to me on this wonderful roller coaster we've created of love, humor, and family.

Thank you for being who you are today and everyday, my sweet baby Rae.

Adam every day you fight and show me what it means to be an authentic father. You have calmed my fears of raising my daughter on multiple occasions.

Watching you alongside Pepper-Sue reminds me that raising my daughter isn't about who the world tells her she should be; rather it's who she tells me she's *going* to be. You're an incredible father and an even better friend. I'm extremely grateful for you and all you have shown me. You are the big brother I never had and I will always love you for that.

To my brothers-in-arms at the 212 Connection Mastermind: James Woosley, Sutton Parks, Robert De Brus, and Randell Mark. Your support, feedback, and encouragement keeps me inspired each week. I'm grateful to have you in my corner.

To James Woosley for helping me publish this book. Thank you for all of your advice and expertise. Your input and impact has not been taken lightly on this project. You are who made me "turn pro." God surely gifted you to me.

To my mother Peggy for being both my mother and my father and having conversations with me that dad simply never could. For reminding me and helping me to realize that smart people have emotions too. Because of you I am better able to share them with Lenox.

Thank you for always believing in me. Although you don't say it, I can see it in your eyes. I will always love you, Mama.

Last but not least a special thank you to my fellow fathers in this book. I pray the collaboration on this project helps share our message with the world. I sincerely thank you for having and sharing your deepest, honest, and most vulnerable *father–daughter conversations* with us.

To each and every father who finds this book in their hands—the ones who take the time to read it and find the courage to implement it. Your daughters need your heart. They need your strength each day. Thank you for finding the power to be the father you were created to be and for having your own *father–daughter conversations.*

—Jason Pockrandt

About the Author

Jason Pockrandt is a transformational life coach, TEDx speaker, author, father, and husband. At only 17-years-old, Jason lost his father to a battle he fought against addiction with prescription pills. It took him eight years to accept the truth his father died and to rediscover his self-worth. Today, it is his personal mission to help you find yours. His main desire is for fatherless fathers worldwide to live a legacy worth leaving for their families and communities.

Connect with Jason

Twitter.com/jasonpockrandt

Facebook.com/jasonpockrandt

Email: jason@jasonpockrandt.com

Watch my TEDx talk, "Fatherless to Fatherhood: The Journey" (bit.ly/fatherlesstedx) or read my first book *The Confident Father's Guidebook: Five Steps to Personal Transformation* (bit.ly/confident).

If you want to learn more about individual one-on-one coaching with me, you can read about the lives I have helped to transform at FatherlessToFatherhood.org.

Call for Reviews

I am extremely grateful for your time and the work that you are putting in to change your life as a husband and father. It means more to me than anything that you are taking strides to give your daughter everything she could ask for in this life. Now I only ask you for one small favor.

Could you take two short minutes and leave an honest review on Amazon? Reviews are the lifeblood of an author, and your support will help this book reach the multitude of fathers who are craving the relationship with their daughters like the one you are about to create.

1:1 Coaching with Jason Pockrandt

If you want to learn more about how I can be your personal guide to transformation and prosperity, I would love to serve you.

Please visit bit.ly/fatherlesscoaching to apply for a coaching session with me.

Until we next connect,

Jason Pockrandt
JasonPockrandt.com

www.ingramcontent.com/pod-product-compliance
Lightning Source LLC
Chambersburg PA
CBHW030105070426
42448CB00037B/972